ELEMENTS OF *Writi*

REVISED EDITION

HOLISTIC SCORING

PROMPTS AND MODELS

► **First Course**

HOLT, RINEHART AND WINSTON

Harcourt Brace & Company

Austin • *New York* • *Orlando* • *Atlanta* • *San Francisco* • *Boston* • *Dallas* • *Toronto* • *London*

Staff Credits

Associate Director: Mescal Evler

Managing Editor: Steve Welch

Project Editors: Susan Sims Britt, Susan Lynch

Editorial Staff: *Editors,* Jonathan David Carson, Adrienne Greer; *Copy Editors,* Joseph S. Schofield IV, Atietie O. Tonwe; *Coordinators,* Susan G. Alexander, Amanda F. Beard, Rebecca Bennett, Wendy Langabeer, Marie Hoffman Price; *Support,* Ruth A. Hooker, Kelly Keeley, Margaret Sanchez, Pat Stover

Design: Christine Schueler

Editorial Permissions: Janet Harrington

Production Coordinator: Rose Degollado

Electronic Publishing Supervisor: Barbara Hudgens

Electronic Publishing Staff: Heather Jernt, *Project Coordinator*
JoAnn Brown, David Hernandez, Rina May Ouellette, Charlie Taliaferro, Ethan Thompson

Contributing Writers

Judith Austin-Mills
Bill Martin
Matthew H. Pangborn
Raymond Teague

Printed in the United States of America

ISBN 0-03-051147-X

1 2 3 4 5 085 00 99 98 97

Contents

To the Teacher

The teacher support provided by the *Annotated Teacher's Edition* is further reinforced by the *Teaching Resources.*

The *Teaching Resources* have been designed to help you in your classroom—where the demands on your time and energy are great—to deal with each student as an individual.

This booklet, *Holistic Scoring: Prompts and Models,* begins with a brief discussion of holistic grading. It contains the Chapter Review Writing Prompts for Chapters 4–10 of the *Pupil's Edition* along with four sample compositions written in response to each prompt. For each of the sample compositions, there is an evaluation and grade.

Holistic Scoring: Prompts and Models is the sixth in a series of eight booklets comprising the *Teaching Resources.*

- *Practicing the Writing Process*
- *Strategies for Writing*
- *Word Choice and Sentence Style*
- *Language Skills Practice and Assessment*
- *Academic and Workplace Skills*
- ***Holistic Scoring: Prompts and Models***
- *Portfolio Assessment*
- *Practice for Assessment in Reading, Vocabulary, and Spelling*

Holistic Scoring

Learning to write is a lot like learning to ride a horse. Both skills can be acquired only through actual experience. No amount of reading about horseback riding will turn a couch potato into an equestrian champion, and no amount of reading about writing will turn students, however bright, into budding Faulkners or Dickinsons.

Teachers have long known, and research has long confirmed, that the best way to learn how to write is to write (and read) frequently. However, asking students to write frequently can create enormous burdens for teachers. Consider, for example, the teacher who has five classes, each with twenty-five students. If each of those 125 students writes one five-paragraph paper, then the teacher will have 625 paragraphs to assess. Is there any wonder that in actual practice many English teachers do not assign writing as often as they feel that they should?

Clearly, it's important for English teachers to develop ways to deal with the paper load that writing instruction creates. One popular method for dealing with this paper load is holistic scoring. Holistic scoring is best understood in contrast to traditional analytic scoring.

Analytic scoring sets up a number of criteria that a composition must meet and then rates the composition according to each of those criteria. For example, a teacher might assign a composition twenty-five points each for content, organization, style, and grammar/usage/mechanics. Traditionally, a teacher would read a composition carefully, mark all its "problems" or "errors," and then subtract points from the predetermined values for each criterion. The many variations on analytic scoring all share this emphasis on criterion-based analysis of components.

When doing holistic scoring, the evaluator likewise sets up distinct criteria on which to judge a composition. However, the evaluator does not assign points or grades for each criterion, and he or she does not mark up the composition. Instead, the evaluator reads the composition and assigns it a single, overall score, often on a scale from 1–4 or from 1–5.

Numerous studies have shown remarkable consistency among the holistic evaluations given by several teachers and between holistic evaluation and analytic evaluation. Given these consistencies, and given the considerable savings in time and effort to be realized by doing holistic evaluation, many educators throughout the country are adopting such evaluation as their primary technique for assessing student writing. The technique is now widely used for evaluating standardized tests of written composition, including tests of minimum competency required for high school graduation in a number of states.

This booklet contains sample compositions based on the **Chapter Review: Writing Prompts** for Chapters 4 through 10. Following each set of writing samples are holistic evaluations of those samples, along with general written comments explaining the evaluations. You might use these writing samples as models or guides for your own holistic grading. You might also choose to make copies of the writing samples to use for classroom lessons or practice activities in evaluating and revising. They can be effectively used for whole class presentations, cooperative group work, or independent practice.

For Further Reading

Cooper, C.R., and L. Odell. *Evaluating Writing.* NCTE, 1977

Elliot, Norbert, Maximino Plata, and Paul Zelhart. *A Program Development Handbook for the Holistic Assessment of Writing.* Lanham, MD: University Press of America, 1990.

Huot, Brian, "Reliability, Validity, and Holistic Scoring: What We Know and What We Need to Know." *College Composition and Communication* 41 (May 1990): 201–213.

Chapter 4: Expressive Writing

Recalling a Childhood Memory

Think of something that happened in your childhood that made you feel proud or happy.
Write a short narrative telling about that event. Use details to make the event come alive.
Make sure to end by telling what the event meant to you.

Understanding the Assignment   Make sure that these statements are true of your
narrative:

1. The introduction grabs the readers' interest.

2. The writer has given enough background information.

3. The events are told in an order that makes sense.

4. The writer has used details that make events, people, and places seem
   real.

5. The outcome and meaning of the experience are clear

6. The story is reasonably free of errors in grammar, usage, mechanics, or
   manuscript form.

Holistic Models: Sample A

Why was the summer after third grade the best summer ever? Because that was when I helped the Cubs won the pennant.

We practiced all spring. We had great pitching and good feilding. But the Eagles, last years champions, had all that plus great batting. I practiced every night after practice, and I practiced all weekend, before games, and after games. My brothers teased me about it, but I knew practice would make the difference. I spent every minute I could at Forestdale Park.

During the season, we had a good record and won all our games except two. We knew we would be in the playoffs. The Eagles thought they would beat us easily, but we proved them wrong.

It was a tight game, but they had us 7-6 in the eighth inning before I got up to bat. Inés was on first base so I knew when that ball went way past the left fielder that I had hit in not just one run but two. We held them at 8-7 for the ninth and that was it. I had brought in the winning runs! I know I have never felt better about anything in my life.

Holistic Models: Sample B

When I was eight my parents let me spend part of the summer on aunt Mary's farm. That was where I learnt to ride a horse.

Smokey was his name, because of his gray color. He also had streaks of white in his tail. I remember how scared I was when I first got on him. I never been on a horse before, and I didn't think they were so big. Smokey was very tall, and he had a very big head and huge teeth. As she lead the horse over the farm path, she told me not to be scared, but I was shaking all over.

Over the weeks, I started taking Smokey further. Sometimes she rode beside me, but sometimes I went alone. I always felt a little scared though. Then one day I was riding along enjoying being out with Smokey and I knew I just wasn't scared anymore. I didn't even know how it happened, but I had learnt to ride. And that felt great! That was the event from my childhood that made me proud and happy.

Holistic Models: Sample C

When I was young I was really good at twirling a baton. I was the youngest one in the class that could usually throw the baton pretty high in the air and catch it. I could turn around while it was in the air and catch it behind my back and I knew some fancy twirls that other kids my age don't know. So I got to represent my class in a show. For my turn on stage I did okay but not really that great. I dropped the baton 2 times. I was SOOO scared!!!!!

I remember when we practiced you could see out to the audience but the night we preformed it was just black out there. That made me really scared. So I didn't do that good. But I remember afterward everybody made such a big fuss about me. My Uncle Hersey gave me flowers. And I got to wear the greatest costume! With white satin and gold sparkles and boots. It was specialest and really really greatest costume there. So that's how I got to be in a baton show at the armery downtown.

Holistic Models: Sample D

I saw a child getting rescued from a burning building. Which made an impression on me. That was what happened to me when I was six.

The building that burned was two blocks over from my house. It was a 2 story condo. We were woked up at about 7 by the sirens. I rember I begged my mom to go see it. When we saw that child being taken out of the building, everyone cheered. A really big crowd was cheering!

The firefighters were at the blaze for about four weeks! They had to keep it from spreading to the other 11 units. I think about 100 families got burned out. Everyone got out okay but the child that was carried by the firefighters. It was in bad shape and had to go to the hospital from the smoke and it almost died for sure. My mom found out about that from Dorothy Sarnowski. She lives on the other end of the same condo.

Holistic Evaluation

Sample A

Rating: 4

Comments: The writer creates interest with a question at the beginning of the narrative. Background information helps make scoring the winning run, the key event, come alive. The events are told in chronological order, and the writer has used details that make the events, people, and places seem real. The outcome and meaning of the experience are clear. The story has only minor errors in grammar, usage, mechanics, or manuscript form.

Sample B

Rating: 3

Comments: This narrative, which provides quite a bit of background information, is in chronological order. The meaning of the experience and its outcome are clear. The details about the place, people, and events seem real, if a little confusing. The opening of this narrative does not create interest. There are also several errors in grammar, usage, and mechanics.

Sample C

Rating: 2

Comments: The subject of this narrative may create some interest in the introduction, but the jumbled order of events makes it difficult to follow what actually happened. Although there are some details that make the people and place seem real, there are not enough. The meaning of the experience is a little vague. There are also many errors in grammar, usage, and mechanics.

Sample D

Rating: 1

Comments: This narrative does not grab the reader's interest. The outcome of the experience is not clear, and there does not seem to be much meaning. Although the details provided might be real, there is not enough background information to make the event come alive or to explain its significance. The narrative also suffers from several errors in grammar, usage, and mechanics.

Chapter 5: Using Description

Describing an Animal

Write a short description of an animal in its usual setting. For example, you might describe a house cat at home or a tiger at the zoo. Describe how the animal looks and sounds. Choose your words carefully so that you can make your reader feel the way you do about the animal.

Understanding the Assignment   Make sure that these statements are true of your description:

1. Details help readers to "see" the subject.

2. The picture is clear.

3. The details create a feeling about the subject.

4. The details are organized in a way that makes sense.

5. The description is reasonably free of errors in grammar, usage, mechanics, or manuscript form.

Holistic Models: Sample A

Every now and then, on a warm summer night, I see an opossum. Sometimes I see it perched on our picket fence. Other times I see it scurry near our shed.

I have never seen an opossum during the day. That's because it hunts at night and must hide somewhere during the day. So I don't see much in the darkness. But here's what I do see.

First, I see a size and shape that's a little like a big rat's size and shape. Next, I notice its small head and pointed nose. Then I see the opossum's eyes, which are big and black. When I look at its body, I know its fur is gray because my dad told me so, but in the moonlight, a possum can look white. The fur is long, about one-half inch. But an opossum is not the kind of animal you want to pet. Part of that is because of its tail. You notice that last, but you don't forget it. It's like a rat's tail, long and hairless.

I think the opossum looks cute in books. But when I am alone at night and I see one, I take two steps back.

Holistic Models: Sample B

Samantha is my grandmother's beautiful black cat. She's black all over except for one white paw. She's small and kind of thin for a cat. She has deep green eyes.

You can usually find Samantha in one place. The big red easy chair in Grandma Pauline's sun porch. That's where Samantha seems to spend practically her entire life. She is usually curled right into a ball there, with a happy look on her face. She sleeps a lot and stretches a lot too. I think that black ball of shiny fur looks beautiful in Grandma's red easy chair.

Samantha is so black that some people don't see her at night. That's when she goes out most of the time. She is thin because she is strong and quick.

Samantha is one of my most favorite cat's because she is so pretty. She is also a friendly cat when she is awake. If you rub her behind her ears, she purrs and purrs. I feel good when I am holding Samantha and petting her. I even wish I had her for my own.

Holistic Models: Sample C

My cocker spaniel Taffy is one of the most loveable little dogs on earth. She is soft, cuddlely, and loveable. She curls up on the rug beside me, as close to me as possible. Sometimes, she just leans up against me, waiting to get petted. I can pet her soft, long fur for ten minutes straight. But the next minute she'll rub up against me again. Begging for more.

Sometimes she begs for food from the table, though. No one in my family likes that. Taffy is pretty smart too. She comes to her name, she can roll over and play dead and can stay, most of the time. She begs for dog bones and my mother's cooking.

Taffy runs away sometimes and gets into trouble. She likes garbage cans. Which is a big problem for everyone. Sometimes she tips them over and makes a big mess. Neighbors call us to complain. Then my dad goes over to clean it up. Taffy is also a little overwieght. From when she runs away and eats everything in sight. Her soft, light brown fur is pretty. That is how she gets the name Taffy.

Holistic Models: Sample D

I have a shark in my aquarium. Hes a great fish. Hes the biggest fish in my tank. He has silver on him. Also black fins, thats his tail. He swims pretty fast. I don't know exacly how fast but hes quick.

The shark is big. Bigger than my other fish. Goldfish, neon fish, and swordtails. Also a catfish on the bottom of the tank. The neon fish are pretty too. Its about the same size as my glass catfish or a little bigger. The sharks alot faster than my glass catfish. Hes faster than the goldfish too. The glass catfish is real interesting to look at, you can see right thru him.

His silver body is very pretty. But maybe the neon fish are the prettiest ones in the tank. Swimming fast and shining. He has big black eyes that look at you. They are on the side of his head. Thats why my shark is the greatest fish in my aquarium.

Holistic Evaluation

Sample A

Rating: 4

Comments: All of the details work very well to enable the reader to "see" the subject. The details are clear and they are organized in a way that makes sense—from what the writer notices first to what the writer notices last. A clear impression of the subject is created, and the description does not contain errors in grammar, usage, mechanics, or manuscript form.

Sample B

Rating: 3

Comments: This student also provides details that enable the reader to "see" the subject. The picture is clear, and the details create a feeling about the subject. The organization doesn't make sense, however. In the first paragraph is a description of what the cat looks like, including her black color and her thinness. These details are returned to in the third paragraph. The description also contains some errors in grammar, usage, and mechanics.

Sample C

Rating: 2

Comments: This description contains some details that help the reader "see" the subject, but the picture is not completely clear. On the one hand, Taffy is a loveable dog, and on the other hand, she gets into trouble, begs, and overeats. The description suffers from lack of organization, especially in the second and third paragraphs. It also contains errors in grammar, usage, and mechanics.

Sample D

Rating: 1

Comments: This description is helpful but not complete in allowing readers to "see" the subject. The writer does convey a sense that the shark is a great fish, but the lack of organization makes it difficult to sort out all the details and to know precisely which ones apply to the shark. The description also suffers from many errors in grammar, usage, and mechanics.

Completing a Story

Some of the best short stories are about events that could never happen in real life. Such stories are called **fantasies.** Think about the following idea for such a short story:

A young boy gets a pet dog as a birthday present. One day, the boy discovers that his dog can talk. The boy is really excited about his discovery and runs to tell his parents. His parents think that he must be imagining things. The dog, meanwhile, refuses to talk when anyone except the boy is around.

In this story, the main character is a young boy. The conflict is that the boy's parents don't believe him. Write an ending for this story. Use your imagination. Give the boy and the dog a name. Create a situation in which the truth about the dog is revealed to everyone.

Understanding the Assignment   Make sure that these statements are true of your story:

1. The conflict is developed.

2. The plot has a strong high point and a satisfying outcome.

3. The characters are lifelike and interesting.

4. The setting is clear. If possible, it creates a mood.

5. The story is reasonably free of errors in grammar, usage, mechanics, or manuscript form.

Holistic Models: Sample A

For many months, my parents tried to talk me out of what they called my "childhood" story. My teacher and the guidance counseler spoke with me about it. Even the principle called me in for "a little chat."

Then one day in late spring, Dad and I took Sheba for a walk together. I could tell Dad was nervous. He kept clearing his throat and looking off across the meadow.

Finally, Dad took a deep breath and said, "Tomás, Mom and I have decided to send you to Brookstone this summer."

"Brookstone?" I shouted. "Isn't that a place for people who have mental problems? You can't be saying this!"

Dad sighed, "We don't like it either. But these crazy ideas have just got to stop. Maybe, someone there …"

His voice trailed off. There was silence for a moment. Then another voice spoke up, a voice that my father was hearing for the first time.

"Yes, it has got to stop," said Sheba.

My father turned white. He looked across the huge, silent meadow. Then he grabbed Sheba's collar. "What was that?" he asked.

My heart pounded when Sheba hesitated. Then she said matter of factly, "This has got to stop."

Holistic Models: Sample B

My parents started to really dislike Thumper. They blamed everything on Thumper. They thought I was making up stories about her so they started being kind of mean to her. They didn't let her sleep inside any more. They let me build a dog house instead. And then I had to start feeding her outside So I stopped telling them about the things she said.

Then one day my mom was all alone in the house. A strange looking man came, he said he was selling encyclopedias. My mom said she wasn't intrested, he said he was comming in anyway. Thumper came running up, bit his leg, and made him howl. He went running, and we never saw him again. About two weeks later, we heard someone in Franklin got robbed by someone selling encyclopedias.

From then on, mom loved Thumper. Once she hugged him and said "Thanks for saving me Thumper". And Thumper replied "Your welcome". Everybody in the room heard it too!

Holistic Models: Sample C

I kept beging Chow to say something to my mom. She wouldn't say a thing. My mom said I was crazy. My dad would walk away if I said a word about what Chow said what a terible summer I had.

This went on and on, Chow kept talking to me but never to mom and dad. I asked her a lot why she wouldn't talk to mom and dad, she never would tell me. That's for me to know was the most she said. My mom kept calling me crazy, my dad got more and more mad about it. One day he got so mad he said he wasn't going to have a catch with me after dinner, we always had a catch after dinner so I knew he was really mad.

But then one day Chow talked. She told my mom she could talk all along, then she told my dad. And so the truth about Chow came out and everyone knew that Chow could talk. So my mom stopped calling me crazy and my dad wasn't mad at me anymore.

Holistic Models: Sample D

So my parents did not believe me. My name is Zachary. My dog's name is Jasmine. She is a mixed dog. Part irish setter and part labrador. She looks like a black irish setter. She is smart like a lab but kind of hyper like a setter. She jumps all over people and scares them even when shes being friendly.

My mom and dad really liked Jasmine alot until I told them she could talk. The first time I said it they just laughed The next time wasn't so funny. After that not funny one bit they said. I knew Jasmine could talk tho. She talked to me everyday and she was my best freind and I told my parents she could really talk but they wouldn't believe me.

One day we brung her to the family picnic and she asked for a hot dog. Plain as day in front of everybody and they were real surprised.

Holistic Evaluation

Sample A

Rating: 4

Comments: The conflict is well developed, and, by means of dialogue and descriptive detail, the characters are made lifelike and interesting. The plot has a strong high point, which is when the voice of Sheba is heard, and a satisfying outcome, which occurs when Sheba repeats herself. The reader can infer that this ends the conflict between the boy and his parents. The setting helps to reinforce the elements of surprise and disbelief. There are only very minor errors in grammar, usage, mechanics, or manuscript form.

Sample B

Rating: 3

Comments: This student also develops and ends the conflict, and the plot has a strong high point and a satisfying outcome. The characters are lifelike and somewhat interesting, although little attention given to the setting. The story contains a few errors in grammar, spelling, and mechanics.

Sample C

Rating: 2

Comments: This story develops and ends the conflict, but it does not have a strong high point or particularly satisfying outcome. Although the characters seem real, there is no sense of setting. The story also has several errors in grammar, usage, and mechanics.

Sample D

Rating: 1

Comments: This review does not develop the conflict. Instead, it restates what was already established. The writer follows the assignment by giving a name to the dog and the boy, but these details are not smoothly integrated in the story. The writer also provides many details that do not belong in the story instead of developing the conflict or providing a satisfying outcome. There is little attention given to making the characters lifelike and no sense of setting. The story also contains many errors in grammar, usage, mechanics, and manuscript form.

Writing a "How-to" Paper

> Write a short "how-to" paper that explains how to do some house-cleaning task. Choose one of the following topics or one of your own:
>
> | | |
> |---|---|
> | How to wash dishes | How to make a bed |
> | How to organize a closet | How to wash windows |
>
> Make sure that your explanation tells what materials are needed and what steps should be taken.

Understanding the Assignment   Make sure that these statements are true of your "how-to" paper:

1. The introduction grabs the reader's attention and gives reasons for learning the process.

2. The paper lists the materials before explaining the first step.

3. All of the necessary steps are included and arranged in chronological order.

4. Transitions help the reader to follow the steps.

5. The paper ends with a conclusion.

6. The paper is reasonably free of errors in grammar, usage, mechanics, or manuscript form.

Holistic Models: Sample A

It's a shame to have to spend a beautiful spring day washing windows. But if you do, you might as well know how to do the job quickly and well.

First, get a ladder, paper towels, window wash liquid, a bucket containing warm soapy water and a sponge, and a radio. If possible, use Cleanest Window Wash liquid, which really works well. Soak It Up paper towels are the best choice for the money. Then turn on the radio to make the job go faster.

Once you are on the ladder ready to wash, size up the window. If it has a lot of dirt or some really dirty spots, use the soapy water and sponge to loosen the dirt, next apply the window wash over the entire surface. The last step is the most important. Wipe the window carefully and thoroughly. If you don't get it all dry, you'll end up with streaks on your window.

Actually, with a little music, a relaxed attitude, and careful wiping, window washing isn't that bad. You can soak up the sun, enjoy the fresh air, and do a job you can be proud of.

Holistic Models: Sample B

Some lucky people have dishwashers. Other unlucky people are dishwashers. If you are one of the unlucky ones, you might find my advice helpful.

First, start with a clean sink. Use clenser to get it clean. Then fill the sink halfway with warm, soapy water. Make the water as warm as is comfortable for your hands.

Begin with the dishes that have the least food on them. Usually the cups and glasses. If you start with dishes that aren't too dirty, the water stays cleaner longer. Wash cups and glasses by running your dishcloth over the entire cup or glass, inside and outside. Then rinse completely with clean water.

Next, do the second most dirty things, such as the plates and silverware. Wash these the same way as the glasses.

Last, do the pots, pans, and baking dishes. Wash these the same as the glasses, accept if there's alot of grease or baked on food. Then you need to use steel wool or clenser to get them clean.

If you do the job right, your dishes will look good. But you will probably have to do the same job tomorrow.

Holistic Models: Sample C

The first thing to do when you wash a sink is take everything off of it and out of it. Take away the soap, the wash cloth, the toothbrushes or anything else laying around on the sink or counter near the sink then take a sponge and wet it. That is important because most cleaners work better when there is water for them to mix up in then put some scowering powder in the sink. You don't need a whole lot of it. Sprinkle a little over the whole sink. Rub the scowering powder on the sink to get the dirt off. If there's dried up toothpaste on the sink, then rub a little harder. Next rinse. Be sure to rinse enough. The sink wont look good if you don't get all the scowering powder off, and scowering powder dries up in white streaks and looks badly if it isn't all rinsed off. For a special touch on sink washing, take a rag and polish up the fawcets, this makes them shine. Then your sink will really sparkle. You can even wash off the counter if there is one.

Holistic Models: Sample D

One thing I can do good is vaccum. Its not such hard work.

All you do is plug the vaccum in and go along the floor. You need to be sure to vaccum the hole floor so you need to move things like the sofa and get behind it and under it. Thats where the best dust is.

If you can't get into a corner or something like that you can use one of the extra peices that goes on the vaccuum. Theres one that looks like a thin tube thats good for corners. You snap that on the vaccuum and just turn it on again.

All you need to vaccum is a little time.

Be sure always to vaccum underneath because even if it looks clean thats where a lot of dirt ends up and your parents can always tell if you didn't do it.

I would rather vaccum than do just about any other housecleaning job. All you need is a vaccum cleaner and a few extra little peices that goes with it.

Holistic Evaluation

Sample A

Rating: 4

Comments: The introduction creates interest and gives a reason for learning the process. The paper also lists the materials before explaining the first step. The steps are in chronological order, and the paper includes all necessary details. Transitions help the reader to follow the steps, and the paper ends with a conclusion. There are only minor errors in grammar, usage, mechanics, or manuscript form.

Sample B

Rating: 3

Comments: The introduction grabs the reader's attention and gives a reason for learning the process. The steps are in chronological order, and the paper includes all necessary details. Transitions help the reader to follow the steps, and there is a witty conclusion. The paper fails to list the materials before explaining the first step, however. Furthermore, there are some errors in grammar, usage, and mechanics.

Sample C

Rating: 2

Comments: This "how-to" paper presents steps in chronological order and includes all necessary details, but it does not list the materials before explaining the first step. It also lacks an interesting introduction and gives no reasons for learning the process. There are some transitions, but no real conclusion. The paper also contains several errors in grammar, usage, mechanics, and manuscript form.

Sample D

Rating: 1

Comments: This "how-to" paper is short on "how-to." It does not introduce the topic by creating interesting or by giving reasons for learning the process. The steps are not in chronological order, and details seem to be missing. There are almost no transitions, and the conclusion is not really a conclusion at all but mere repetition. The paper also contains many errors in grammar, usage, and mechanics.

Chapter 8: Writing to Persuade

Writing a Radio Advertisement

You are a copywriter for an advertising agency. Write a thirty-second public service radio ad. In the ad, try to persuade teenagers to eat healthy foods instead of junk foods. Make sure that your ad presents an opinion and supports it.

Note: If you wish to do so, you can add sound effects to your ad. To indicate a sound effect, use parentheses and the abbreviation SFX, as follows:

> Tired of rush hour traffic jams? (SFX: Automobile horns) Try traveling by metro bus. (SFX: Sound of bus stopping)

Understanding the Assignment   Make sure that these statements are true of your ad:

1. The beginning grabs the listener's attention.

2. The ad clearly states an opinion.

3. The ad presents enough supporting material to convince the audience.

4. The ad does not contain incorrect or misleading statements.

5. The ending is strong.

6. The ad is reasonably free of errors in grammar, usage, mechanics, or manuscript form.

Holistic Models: Sample A

Imagine your own heart. (SFX: the sound of a heart beating) Now imagine that heart with a big thick layer of hard white fat around it. (SFX: the sound of a heart beating more slowly) Why is it beating slower? Because fat that has built up in the arteries is making it difficult for the blood to move through the body. Fat from overeating. Fat from eating the wrong foods. Fat from foods like french fries, chips, the wrong kinds of cooking oils, butter, and red meats. That kind of fat can bring your heart to a stop. A dead stop.

You might think you are young and your heart is healthy, but did you know that fat deposits start to form when you are young? Well, they do. And one way these deposits can form is through diet. When you choose fatty snacks and other junk food instead of fruits and vegetables, you give these deposits a chance to form. And over the years they build up. Until one day … (SFX: sound of a heart barely beating and then not beating at all)

Holistic Models: Sample B

Voice 1: I'm having trouble running. I guess its this wieght. I can't do some of the things I use to. And I guess I don't feel so great about myself either.

Voice 2: Well, I have been noticing that you are looking badly. And I think I know why. It's those chips and sodas at lunch and after school every day. Maybe you should cut it out. Start snacking on fruit instead.

Narrator: Of course he should cut it out. Chips are loaded with unhealthy fats and salt and soda often contains well over 100 empty calories.

Voice 1: I sure would like to be able to run a mile again…

(Pause)

Narrator: You *can* run that mile, by cutting down on fats and sugar. Your body needs health food, not junk food. The choice is your's.

Holistic Models: Sample C

So, your filling up on junk food? Your eating a lot of salty, fat foods with lots of calories and no vitamins? If you are you got to change now. Its time to cut the junk and chose whats healthy.

You can look and feel like a movie star if you just cut fats out of your diet starting now. Throw away all the foods in your house that contains fat and the next thing you know you'll be on you're way to an all new you. Some foods that you think are healthy for you, like cheese, can have fat in it, so don't get fooled.

(SFX: sound of things being thrown into the trash) Thats right. Just get rid of the fat and watch yourself change. Sheila watched herself change, Martin watched hisself change. Now its you're turn.

Holistic Models: Sample D

This is a public service announcement, that is about food. Theres 2 kinds. Good food and junk food. Teenagers eat too much junk food and not enough good food. They need to start turning that around backwards and eating more good food and less junk food. This is easy to do if you only think about it. Like when they pack there lunch. There things you can pick and there things you can't and there old enough to know the difference. Of course some things are not so bad as you think. They say potato chips is bad but when you look at the label you see theirs some protein in them, a little bit, and some vitamins too. So some junk foods are not all junk. You can look at almost any chips and see theres some good stuff in them even though there junk food.

Holistic Evaluation

Sample A

Rating: 4

Comments: This ad has a strong beginning that grabs the listener's attention, and the sound effects are used very well at both the beginning and the end of the ad. The ad clearly states an opinion and presents enough supporting material to convince the audience. There are no incorrect or misleading statements, and the ending is dramatic. Although there are several fragments in the ad, they are used effectively, and there are no major errors in grammar, usage, mechanics, or manuscript form.

Sample B

Rating: 3

Comments: Although this ad does not create interest at the beginning, it clearly states an opinion. The ad presents enough supporting material to convince the audience, and it does not contain incorrect or misleading statements. It has a strong ending, and the use of different voices and a narrator reflects some originality and care in creating the ad. There are a few errors in grammar, usage, and mechanics.

Sample C

Rating: 2

Comments: This ad starts with a question that might create some interest on the part of the listener, and it clearly states an opinion. Nevertheless, the ad lacks enough supporting information to persuade an audience, and there are several incorrect and misleading statements in the ad. There are also many errors in grammar, usage, and mechanics.

Sample D

Rating: 1

Comments: This ad does not grab the listener's attention. It also does not clearly state an opinion or present enough material to convince the audience. The ending is very weak, and the ad contains numerous errors in grammar, usage, and mechanics.

Chapter 9: Writing About Literature

Writing About a Television Character

You are a television critic for a teen magazine. Choose a main character from a television program and write a review of that character. In your review, give the name of the program and tell whether the character is believable or entertaining. Present evidence to support your opinion of the character.

Understanding the Assignment   Make sure that these statements are true of your review:

1. The introduction identifies the television program and the character's name.

2. The introduction states the writer's opinion of the character.

3. The body presents details from the television program to back up the writer's opinion of the character.

4. The conclusion restates the main idea of the review.

5. The review is reasonably free of errors in grammar, usage, mechanics, or manuscript form.

Holistic Models: Sample A

The character of Joe Nevada on EBS's *Precinct 7* is one of the most interesting and believable characters on television this season. Nevada is a tough cop who is a real person to.

In one of the first shows, Nevada makes a mistake and looses an important suspect he's supposed to be tailing. He immediately reports his mistake. At night, when he's home, he feels miserable, and the viewer feels sorry for Nevada because he is such a responsible person.

In a recent show, Nevada missed someone he fired at. This is a believable detail. On almost every other police show on television, the hero never misses a shot.

In last week's show, Nevada had the courage to help a fellow officer who had been breaking the law. Nevada admitted that he once had the same problem himself. This shows that Nevada is an everyday guy who makes mistakes, yet he knows right from wrong.

Joe Nevada is likable and believable because he acts like a regular guy who happens to be a good police officer, too. You should watch *Precinct 7* on Tuesdays at 9 P.M. just to see him.

Holistic Models: Sample B

Penelope Stern is a doctor on *Ellis Hospital.* She is one of the most entertaining doctors ever on television.

Dr. Stern always greets her patients with some kind of joke. She can go up to someone's bedside that is really suffering and make him smile. On one show, she ended up dancing with an old guy that was in the hospital after having a stroke. The first time he got up it was to laugh and dance with Dr. Stern. Dr. Stern is respected by the other doctors in the hospital too. She makes jokes with them during surgery. She even plays jokes on them in the cafeteria. Mixing up there orders, putting soup in there milk, and doing other crazy things that make you laugh. No one can get through one show without laughing at least once.

She also makes the patients who are really scared laugh a little, that helps them get through being in the hospital. Some of the jokes are a little silly sometimes, and you might not think all of them are funny.

Holistic Models: Sample C

Henry Sanchez is a lawyer on the show *Ramírez and Sons*. That's the new show about law and lawyers on Tuesday nights at eight, and Sanchez is the most humorous character.

Henry Sanchez is really good looking, as you would expect. He is about six feet tall with an atheletic build. He wears great clothes. In the courtroom he always has the best arguments. He can out-argue any attorny whose against him. Usually whose against him is women. These women are usually all good looking too. At the end of the court case, Sanchez usually ends up going out on a date with them. They usually don't seem to mind even if they did lose the case. Even though Sanchez has only just started off in the law firm of Ramírez and Sons, you can tell he is probably going to become a boss fast. Mr. Ramírez really likes him like a son and gives him a lot of the tough cases and the ones that could make the firm a lot of money. The younger Ramírez children, two sons and a daughter, are really good lawyers. They win most every case too. But Sanchez is the one I like.

Holistic Models: Sample D

Last night, Cassy Roosevelt really made me angry. She is the meanest, most rotten daughter that parents could ever have. She was planning to run away with her mother's little dog, Jazz, and enter him in a beauty contest for dogs. Her mother was so upset, she called the whole town of Parkersville, including the police, the hospital, the veterinarian and the fire station. On "The Roosevelts" Cassy is always the one making trouble. One time she had so many bad grades on her report card the principle had to call up her mom and have her come into school regular. They had to make and follow a special study plan just for Cassy. Who didn't have the sense to follow it. Cassy is real different from her brothers, who are both A students and stars on the football and chess teams. Mr. and Mrs. Roosevelt are always discussing Cassy and what they are going to do with her, and week after week she is the worse daughter any family could have.

Holistic Evaluation

Sample A

Rating: 4

Comments: In this clearly written review, the introduction identifies the television program and the character's name. It also states the writer's opinion of the character. The body presents details from the program to back up the writer's opinion of the character, and the conclusion restates the main idea of the review. The review contains only minor errors in grammar, usage, mechanics, or manuscript form.

Sample B

Rating: 3

Comments: This student also states the character's name and the name of the television program in the introduction, and the introduction also states the student's opinion of the character. The body presents details from the program to back up the writer's opinion of the character. The review lacks a conclusion, however. It also contains errors in grammar, usage, and mechanics.

Sample C

Rating: 2

Comments: The introduction identifies the character and the television program, but it does not state the writer's opinion of the character. The body includes details from the program that explain some of the things that happen on the show and why the writer likes the character, but not all of them support the main idea that the character is humorous. There is no conclusion, and there are several errors in grammar, usage, and mechanics.

Sample D

Rating: 1

Comments: This review does not contain an introduction, and the reader does not know which television program is being referred to until well into the review. The writer states an opinion, but it is not clear at the outset what that opinion is. The details that tell about the show provide a mixture of support for the opinion and unrelated ideas. There are also many errors in grammar, usage, mechanics, and manuscript form.

Name _____ Date _____ Class _____

Writing a Paragraph for a Report

You are writing a report on current events around the world. Each paragraph of the report will summarize a major event. Write one paragraph for that report. To write your paragraph, first choose a current event that you want to write about. Then find two sources of information about the event. For example, you could use a newspaper article and a television or radio news report. Use the two sources in your paragraph. Quote one of your sources and paraphrase the other.

Understanding the Assignment   Make sure that these statements are true of your paragraph:

1. The paragraph uses at least two different sources of information.

2. The paragraph contains enough information to make the event clear to the reader.

3. Most of the paragraph is written in its writer's own words.

4. Quotation marks show when someone else is being quoted.

5. The first sentence of the paragraph introduces the subject.

6. The information in the paragraph is clearly organized.

7. The paragraph has a conclusion.

8. The sources of information are listed at the end of the paragraph.

9. The paragraph is reasonably free of errors in grammar, usage, mechanics, or manuscript form.

Holistic Models: Sample A

Pineapples from Hawaii will soon be hard to find at the supermarket. The State that once was known for its pineapples will soon be going out of the pineapple business. As Robert T. Rheinhold wrote in the *New York Times,* "over the next 18 months, crews will harvest the last planting on this island, once the largest pineapple plantation in the world." A report on National Public Radio explained that Hawaiian pineapples are no longer profitable. Developers feel they can make more money by using Hawaii's land for hotels. Pineapples grown in Asia can be sold at a lower price than those grown in Hawaii. That's why the pineapple growing days of Hawaii are rapidly coming to a close.

Sources: *New York Times,* National Public Radio

Holistic Models: Sample B

Can the break up of the Soviet Union mean that American companies are going to make a fortune? It is true American companies are now turning their eyes on the new teritories of the Soviet Union. They hope to find new business opportunities. The *Chicago Tribune* says that "companies are already signing risky deals." Some people think these companies are acting too fast! A reporter on Channel WRPB, Cincinnati, said that "the excitement of a rich land with great investment opporunities is tempting many business people to act too quickly." He said that "Caution is advised until the situation is stable." No one says for sure when that will be.

Sources: *Chicago Tribune*, WRPB

Holistic Models: Sample C

The people who run Euro Disneyland have a strick dress code, it applies to clothing, makeup, jewelery, hair styles. And many other things about a persons appearence. If you don't follow it you can't be hired. If you are hired and you don't follow it, you can be fired. There was a report on CBS News last night about arguments between the French people and the people who run Euro Disneyland. Which is like Disney World, but it is in France. The French people say this dress code is ridiculous, maybe it is even against the law. Euro Disneyland leaders say that how people dress is important for the company and for the theme park.

Source: CBS News

Holistic Models: Sample D

Every year there are more and more people without any place to live, they are the homeless people, and we need to start thinking about them. Some of them sleeps on the sidewalks and some of them sleeps on trains and in train stations. They dress in rags. They do not have enough food to eat. They have to beg. There are some shelters but not enough, the problem keeps growing and growing. Another big problem in the newspaper is the energy crisis. All the big cities have more homeless people than they can handle. You can see them all over the place, and it is really sad to see them in the freezing weather, and you wonder where they will go at night. This is the single most compelling issue of our decade. The problem is worser and worser all the time. Education is another problem in the newspaper.

Holistic Evaluation

Sample A

Rating: 4

Comments: This paragraph uses two sources of information and contains enough information to make the event clear to the reader. The paragraph is written in its writer's own words, except for the quotation. The first sentence introduces the subject, the information is clearly organized, and there is a conclusion. The sources of information are listed at the end of the paragraph, and there are no errors in grammar, usage, mechanics, or manuscript form.

Sample B

Rating: 3

Comments: This paragraph uses two sources of information. The first sentence introduces the subject, there is enough information to make the issue clear, and the paragraph ends logically. Most of the paragraph appears to be in the writer's own words, but the writer is a bit confused about when and how to quote. Sources are listed at the end of the paragraph. The paragraph contains a few errors in grammar, usage, and mechanics.

Sample C

Rating: 2

Comments: The paragraph presents enough information to make the event clear, and the the paragraph is in its writer's own words. However, the first sentence does not introduce the subject, and the information is not as clearly organized as it should be. The paragraph uses only one source of information instead of two. The conclusion is logical, but the paragraph suffers from several errors in grammar, usage, and mechanics.

Sample D

Rating: 1

Comments: This paragraph tends to persuade more than to report. It does not appear to use or list any sources. Although most of the paragraph seems to be in its writer's own words, the sentence that reads "This is the single most compelling issue of our decade" is so different from the rest of the paragraph that it seems to have been copied without quotation marks. The conclusion of this paragraph veers off in a new direction, as does one of the sentences in the middle of the paragraph; as a result, the information is not clearly organized. There are also many errors in grammar, usage, and mechanics.